ALL ABOUT THE RODEO

THE RODEO

Lynn Stone

Rourke
Publishing LLC
Vero Beach, Florida 32964

www.rourkepublishing.com

Photo credits:
Front cover © Eric Limon, back cover © Olivier Le Queinec, all other photos © Tony Bruguiere except page 5 © lightasafeather, page 17 © Dennis Oblander, page 24/25 courtesy of to Western History Collections, University of Oklahoma Libraries, page 26 courtesy of the Library of Congress

Editor: Jeanne Sturm

Cover and page design by Nicola Stratford, Blue Door Publishing

Library of Congress Cataloging-in-Publication Data

Stone, Lynn M.
  The rodeo / Lynn M. Stone.
      p. cm. -- (All about the rodeo)
  Includes index.
  ISBN 978-1-60472-387-8
  1. Rodeos--Juvenile literature. I. Title.
  GV1834.S86 2009
  791.8'4--dc22
                                        2008018783

Printed in the USA

CG/CG

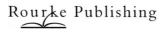

Rourke Publishing

www.rourkepublishing.com – rourke@rourkepublishing.com
Post Office Box 3328, Vero Beach, FL 32964

Table Of Contents

The Rodeo

Rodeo is more than a sport. It is a collection of sports under a single banner. The major rodeo events are divided into two groups: **roughstock**, or judged, events, and timed events.

★ Bareback riding, saddle **bronc** riding, and bull riding are the major roughstock events. Judging and time both play a role in roughstock competition. Steer wrestling, barrel racing, tie-down roping, and team roping are the standard timed events. Some rodeos feature additional events, such as goat tying, breakaway roping, and pole racing. The National Little Britches Rodeo Association **sponsors** 13 rodeo events for boys and girls ages 5 through 18.

Rodeo brings into the 21st century a tradition of cowboy life on the American range. Indeed, some of the main rodeo events evolved from real cowboy chores on western ranches.

Rodeo, of course, is not exactly a replica of life on the range. But rodeo does recreate some of the mystique of the western cowboy's life, of dark nights and bright stars, of galloping horses and wayward cattle. Like range riding itself, rodeo is a blend of leather and livestock, dirt and denim, and competition both fierce and fair.

Cowboys were climbing aboard bucking horses long before the rodeo began.

Stirrups, chaps, boots, saddle leather, and rope join forces on a saddle bronc ride.

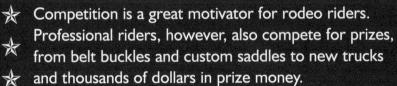

⭐ Competition is a great motivator for rodeo riders.
⭐ Professional riders, however, also compete for prizes,
  from belt buckles and custom saddles to new trucks
⭐ and thousands of dollars in prize money.

Rodeo Organizations

Major rodeos are operated by organizations that oversee **venues**, guidelines for events, animal welfare, and every other aspect of the sport. These organizations help attract large corporate sponsors. If you attend a rodeo, you will see the names of well known companies plastered on arena walls and even on the clothing worn by the rodeo participants. Sponsors increase the amount of prize money.

★ The oldest and largest of rodeo organizations is the Professional Rodeo Cowboys Association (**PRCA**). A few other major organizations are the Professional Bull Riders (PBR), the National Intercollegiate Rodeo Association, the Women's Professional Rodeo Association (WPRA), the National Barrel Horse Association, National Little Britches Rodeo Association, and the National High School Rodeo Association.

The Greeley Independence Stampede is a PRCA rodeo in Colorado.

Competitors

Rodeo competitors are athletes, as are the animals they rope and ride. Rodeo athletes are stocked with courage, along with the athlete's usual checklist: stamina, strength, agility, coordination, and the ability to think quickly and clearly.

Most rodeo competitors are from western states, which have a long tradition of ranching and rodeos.

Women and men do not typically compete against each other in the same events, nor do children compete against adults. Women barrel racers, for example, compete against other women.

The majority of rodeo cowgirls compete only in barrel racing, and barrel races at major rodeos are events for women only. Still, barrel racing is not entirely a women's sport, any more than bull riding is strictly a men's.

o has had numerous stars, but
aps none has been more
ordinary than Ty Murray.
ay won seven All-Around
d Championship titles, earning
ickname *King of the Cowboys*.
tarred at bareback, saddle
c, and bull riding. In 1993, at
ars of age, Murray became the
gest millionaire in rodeo
ry. He also was a founder of
BR.

Riding a bull requires great athletic ability – as does being a bucking bull!

Larry Mahan was another remarkable rodeo athlete. He won five consecutive All-Around World Championship titles between 1966 and 1970 and picked up a sixth in 1973. He rode in 1,200 rodeos without having any major injuries. He retired in 1977 at age 34.

The Rodeo Venue

Rodeos are held in large indoor or outdoor arenas with dirt floors surrounded by a wall or fence. The size of the arenas varies both in seating capacity and the square footage of the arena floor itself.

Spectators watch from bleachers around and above the rodeo arena.

Rodeos are most popular in the western states, but rodeos are held in almost every part of the United States and in parts of Canada. Mexico, Brazil, Argentina, and Australia also have rodeos, although they are not exact copies of American rodeos in style or events.

The largest and best known rodeos in North America

- ★ The Calgary Stampede (Calgary, Alberta)
- ★ Cheyenne Frontier Days (Cheyenne, Wyoming)
- ★ The Dodge National Circuit Finals Rodeo (Pocatello, Idaho)
- ★ Professional Bull Riders' Built Tough World Finals (Las Vegas)
- ★ National Finals Rodeo (Las Vegas, Nevada)
- ★ National Western Rodeo (Denver, Colorado)
- ★ Southwest Exposition Livestock and Rodeo (Fort Worth, Texas)
- ★ La Fiesta de Los Vaqueros (Tucson, Arizona).

PRCA's annual National Finals Rodeo is held in Las Vegas.

Saddle Bronc Riding

Saddle bronc riding is sometimes called rodeo's classic event. A saddle bronc rider mounts a horse that has never been trained for riding. The rider's goal is to stay mounted for eight seconds, during which time the rider may grasp the rein with one hand only. The rider must also perform within a strict set of style guidelines.

A bronc hurtles upward in an attempt to throw its rider.

Bareback Bronc Riding

A bareback bronc rider also tries to stay aboard for eight seconds. During that time, the rider earns style points by the way in which he uses his spurs. The horse is also judged, and the total points earned by the rider and the horse become the rider's final score.

A cowboy has no more than a handle, called a rigging, to grasp on his wild bareback ride.

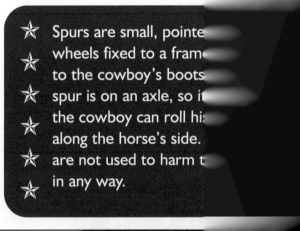

★ Spurs are small, pointe
★ wheels fixed to a fram
   to the cowboy's boots
★ spur is on an axle, so i
   the cowboy can roll hi
   along the horse's side.
★ are not used to harm t
★ in any way.

Bull Riding

Danger rides with every rodeo competitor who sits atop or attempts to manhandle a large animal. The most dangerous event for a cowboy is bull riding. A bull rider climbs aboard a horned bull that typically weighs 1,750 pounds (795 kilograms). First, the bull rider attempts to stay on the bucking bull for eight seconds. If he completes the eight seconds, he is judged on both his performance and the bull's. If the rider is tossed before eight seconds have passed, he earns no points.

Cheyenne Frontier

A bucking horse usually has no interest in kicking its fallen rider. A bull, however, is a different beast. A bull often shows a keen interest in trying to **gore** the rider who just fell off its back. Rodeo bullfighters, sometimes called rodeo clowns, bravely distract the bucking bull while the cowboy makes his escape from the arena.

A bull rider sits briefly atop nearly a ton of tossing might.

Steer Wrestling

Steer wrestling, also known as bulldogging, is another highly demanding and dangerous sport. A steer wrestler attempts to move from the back of his running horse to the head and back of a running steer. With brute strength, agility, and leverage, the steer wrestler first has to grip the steer's horns with his arms. In almost the same motion, he must bring himself and the animal to a stop and flip the steer onto its side. The best steer wrestlers can accomplish the feat in fewer than six seconds.

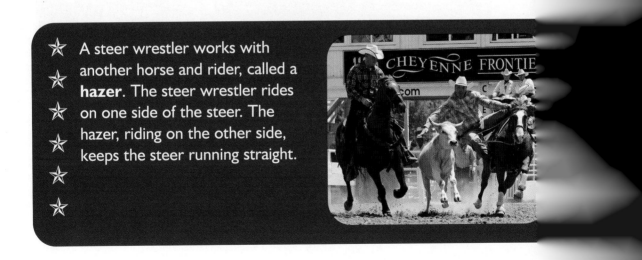

A steer wrestler works with another horse and rider, called a **hazer**. The steer wrestler rides on one side of the steer. The hazer, riding on the other side, keeps the steer running straight.

Barrel Racing

Barrel racers are highly skilled riders, usually women, who race in a cloverleaf pattern around three barrels arranged in a triangle. The first two barrels, at the base of the triangle, are 90 feet (27 meters) apart. The third barrel, at the triangle point, is 105 feet (32 meters) from the other two.

Quick turns equal quick times for a barrel racer.

The idea is to race quickly to each barrel, loop around it, and streak back to the finish line. If a rider or horse strikes a barrel, the rider is charged with a penalty of five seconds.

A barrel racer streaks toward the finish line.

Tie-Down Roping

Tie-down roping, once known as calf roping, is a contest against the clock. It matches riding, roping, and tying skills. Using a rope with one end attached to the saddle, the cowboy on horseback tosses the rope to loop a running calf around its neck. The horse comes to an abrupt stop, and the cowboy dismounts and runs to the calf. He flips the standing calf over and quickly ropes any three legs. Meanwhile, the cowboy's horse puts enough pressure on the rope to keep the calf in place without dragging it.

A tie-down roper rushes to a roped calf.

Team Roping

Team roping involves two cowboys and their horses in pursuit of a steer. The cowboy in the lead, called a **header**, ropes a steer. Still mounted, the cowboy and horse turn the steer so that its hind legs face the second cowboy, called a **heeler**. The heeler, who also remains mounted, loops the hind legs of the kicking steer. The clock stops when the cowboys' ropes are taut and their two horses face each other.

Team ropers subdue a young steer.

Rodeo History

The war between Mexico and the United States (1846 -1848) resulted in much of the Southwest and what is now California becoming American territory. As more and more Americans rushed into the West after America's Civil War (1861-1865), many of them created large cattle ranches. The new American ranchers and

s like this of cowboys in the est rapidly disappeared by art of the 20th century.

cowboys learned some of their horsemanship and ranching skills from the Spanish cowboys (*vaqueros*) who had lived in the southwest for many generations before the tide of American settlers. Cowboys learned how to rope, herd cattle, break horses, and brand calves.

Eventually the cowboys' skills became a source of competition between ranches. Legend has it that the first informal rodeo took place on July 4, 1869, in Deer Trail, Colorado, a competition between cowboys from neighboring ranches. It's likely that similar events had occurred between *vaqueros* on Spanish ranches in Mexico and in the American Southwest in earlier years.

★ The first formal rod
★ probably occurred i
   in Cheyenne, Wyom
★ That event became
   ancestor of today's
   Cheyenne Frontier
★ the granddaddy of
★ American rodeos.

The Old West was slipping away by the 1890s. By then the railroads were expanding. Cowboys no longer had to drive cattle to distant markets. The grand cattle drives on the legendary Santa Fe and Chisholm Trails ended. Electricity had arrived and automobiles were not far behind. American life was rapidly changing, and the cowboy life was fading fast.

Buffalo Bill Cody was a former buffalo hunter and Indian fighter, but he turned **entrepreneur**. He started a rodeo in North Platte, Nebraska, in 1882. Soon after, he founded Buffalo Bill's Wild West Show. The show glamorized the Old West with cowboy competitions, costumed Indians, Annie Oakley's demonstrations of marksmanship, and a circus atmosphere. Cody's show and those of several imitators, like Pawnee Bill, gave the American rodeo its modern roots.

Although now they are primarily sport, rodeos have kept an element of showmanship.

The Wild West shows disappeared, but the competitions between cowboys did not. Those competitions became the rodeo, a word coined from a similar Spanish word that meant *round up* or *surround*.

Many western towns embraced rodeo events, turning them into local festivals. As rodeo popularity blossomed, organizers worked to establish standard guidelines and associations to govern events and give rodeo competitors a powerful voice.

Entrepreneurs like Buffalo Bill, Pawnee Bill, and Gene Autry, the singing cowboy, are gone, but part of their legacy is a flourishing sport. The largest of the rodeo organizations, the PRCA, **sanctions** over 700 rodeos each year. Meanwhile, competitors from a new generation await their chance to win the supreme prize – a gold buckle.

Cheyenne, Wyoming's Cheyenne Frontier Days rodeo bills itself as the "Daddy of 'em All."

Glossary

bronc (brongk): referring to a bucking horse

entrepreneur (on-tru-pru-NUR): one who begins a business

gore (GOR): to injure with a sharp object, especially with an animal's horn

hazer (HAYZ-ur): a mounted cowboy whose job is to keep a steer running in a straight line during rodeo steer wrestling competition

header (HED-ur): a mounted cowboy who ropes a steer's head in rodeo team roping competition

heeler (HEEL-ur): a mounted cowboy who ropes a steer's hind legs in rodeo team roping competition

PRCA (PRCA): the Professional Rodeo Cowboys Association, the oldest and largest of rodeo organizations

roughstock (RUHF-stok): referring to a rodeo's judged events with broncos and bulls

sanctions (SANGK-shuhnz): gives permission and official recognition to an event

sponsors (SPON-surz): when a person or group pays to make an event happen

venues (VEN-yooz): places where activities are held

Further Reading

Want to learn more about rodeos? The following books and websites are a great place to start!

Books

Ehringer, Gavin. *Rodeo Legends: 20 Extraordinary Athletes of America's Sport*. Western Horseman, 2003.

Mahoney, Silvia Gann. *College Rodeo: From Show to Sport*. Texas A & M University Press, 2004.

Presnall, Judith Jada. *Rodeo Animals*. Gale Group, 2004.

Websites

http://www.wpra.com
http://prorodeo.org
http://nbha.com
www.nlbra.com

Index

About The Author

Lynn M. Stone is a widely published wildlife and domestic animal photographer and the author of more than 500 children's books. His book *Box Turtles* was chosen as Outstanding Science Trade Book and Selectors' Choice for 2008 by the Science Committee of the National Science Teachers' Association and the Children's Book Council.